A LOOK AT THE BILL OF RIGHTS

The Right to DUE PROCESS

BY MARY GRIFFIN

CRASHCOURSE

Gareth Stevens PUBLISHING

Please visit our website, www.garethstevens.com. For a free color catalog of all our high-quality books, call toll free 1-800-542-2595 or fax 1-877-542-2596.

Library of Congress Cataloging-in-Publication Data
Names: Griffin, Mary, 1978- author.
Title: The right to due process / Mary Griffin.
Description: Buffalo : Gareth Stevens Publishing, 2026. | Series: A look at the bill of rights | Includes index.
Identifiers: LCCN 2024033793 | ISBN 9781482470383 (library binding) | ISBN 9781482470376 (paperback) | ISBN 9781482470390 (ebook)
Subjects: LCSH: Due process of law–United States–Juvenile literature.
Classification: LCC KF4765 .G75 2026 | DDC 347.73/5–dc23/eng/20240725
LC record available at https://lccn.loc.gov/2024033793

First Edition

Published in 2026 by
Gareth Stevens Publishing
2544 Clinton Street
Buffalo, NY 14224

Designer: Andrea Davison-Bartolotta
Editor: Kristen Rajczak Nelson

Photo credits: Cover, p. 1 MR.Yanukit/Shutterstock.com; series art (interior background texture) Nik Merkulov/Shutterstock.com; series art (fact box sticker) Sulovsky/Shutterstock.com; series art (blue backgrounds) Le Chernina/Shutterstock.com; series art (banners) saicle/Shutterstock.com; p. 5 courtesy of the National Archives; p. 7 duncan1890/iStockphoto.com; p. 9 (house, people) DESING CREATOR/Shutterstock.com; p. 9 (liberty bell) sada jiwa/Shutterstock.com; p. 9 (main) Yuriy K/Shutterstock.com; p. 10 Karkhut/Shutterstock.com; p. 11 Michael Muller/Shutterstock.com; p. 12 Nate Hovee/Shutterstock.com; p. 13 Everett Collection/Shutterstock.com; p. 15 wavebreakmedia/Shutterstock.com; pp. 17, 29 (top) sirtravelalot/Shutterstock.com; p. 19 Fedor Selivanov/Shutterstock.com; p. 20 Inkoly/Shutterstock.com; p. 21 PeopleImages.com - Yuri A/Shutterstock.com; p. 23 (top) fizkes/Shutterstock.com; p. 23 (bottom) Noel V. Baebler/Shutterstock.com; p. 25 File:Judge Henry Friendly.jpg/Wikimedia Commons; p. 27 fast-stock/Shutterstock.com; p. 29 (bottom) Natee Meepian/Shutterstock.com; p. 30 Blackboard/Shutterstock.com.

Printed in China

CPSIA compliance information: Batch #QS26GS: For further information contact Gareth Stevens at 1-800-542-2595.

Contents

Words in the glossary appear in **bold** type the first time they are used in the text.

THE BILL OF RIGHTS

The Bill of Rights is the first 10 amendments to the U.S. Constitution. It lists rights that are **guaranteed** to U.S. citizens, or those who live legally in the country. The right to due process is part of the Bill of Rights.

Make the GRADE

A constitution is the basic laws by which a country or state is governed. An amendment is a change made to a constitution.

We the People of the United States, in Order to form a more perfect Union, establish Justice,
insure domestic Tranquility, provide for the common defence, promote the general Welfare, and secure the Blessings of Liberty to ourselves
and our Posterity, do ordain and establish this Constitution for the United States of America.

Article. I.

Section. 1. All legislative Powers herein granted shall be vested in a Congress of the United States, which shall consist of a Senate and House
of Representatives.

Section. 2. The House of Representatives shall be composed of Members chosen every second Year by the People of the several States, and the Electors
in each State shall have the Qualifications requisite for Electors of the most numerous Branch of the State Legislature.

No Person shall be a Representative who shall not have attained to the Age of twenty five Years, and been seven Years a Citizen of the United States,
and who shall not, when elected, be an Inhabitant of that State in which he shall be chosen.

Representatives and direct Taxes shall be apportioned among the several States which may be included within this Union, according to their respective
Numbers, which shall be determined by adding to the whole Number of free Persons, including those bound to Service for a Term of Years, and excluding Indians
not taxed, three fifths of all other Persons. The actual Enumeration shall be made within three Years after the first Meeting of the Congress of the United States,
and within every subsequent Term of ten Years, in such Manner as they shall by Law direct. The Number of Representatives shall not exceed one for every
thirty Thousand, but each State shall have at Least one Representative; and until such enumeration shall be made, the State of New Hampshire shall be
entitled to chuse three, Massachusetts eight, Rhode Island and Providence Plantations one, Connecticut five, New York six, New Jersey four, Pennsylvania
eight, Delaware one, Maryland six, Virginia ten, North Carolina five, South Carolina five, and Georgia three.

When vacancies happen in the Representation from any State, the Executive Authority thereof shall issue Writs of Election to fill such Vacancies.

The House of Representatives shall chuse their Speaker and other Officers; and shall have the sole Power of Impeachment.

Section. 3. The Senate of the United States shall be composed of two Senators from each State, chosen by the Legislature thereof, for six Years; and each
Senator shall have one Vote.

Immediately after they shall be assembled in Consequence of the first Election, they shall be divided as equally as may be into three Classes. The Seats
of the Senators of the first Class shall be vacated at the Expiration of the second Year, of the second Class at the Expiration of the fourth Year, and of the third
Class at the Expiration of the sixth Year, so that one third may be chosen every second Year; and if Vacancies happen by Resignation, or otherwise, during the
Recess of the Legislature of any State, the Executive thereof may make temporary Appointments until the next Meeting of the Legislature, which shall then fill
such Vacancies.

No Person shall be a Senator who shall not have attained to the Age of thirty Years, and been nine Years a Citizen of the United States, and who shall
not, when elected, be an Inhabitant of that State for which he shall be chosen.

The Vice President of the United States shall be President of the Senate, but shall have no Vote, unless they be equally divided.

The Senate shall chuse their other Officers, and also a President pro tempore, in the Absence of the Vice President, or when he shall exercise the Office of
President of the United States.

The Senate shall have the sole Power to try all Impeachments. When sitting for that Purpose, they shall be on Oath or Affirmation. When the President
of the United States is tried, the Chief Justice shall preside: And no Person shall be convicted without the Concurrence of two thirds of the Members present.

Judgment in Cases of Impeachment shall not extend further than to removal from Office, and disqualification to hold and enjoy any Office of honor,
Trust or Profit under the United States: but the Party convicted shall nevertheless be liable and subject to Indictment, Trial, Judgment and Punishment,
according to Law.

Section. 4. The Times, Places and Manner of holding Elections for Senators and Representatives, shall be prescribed in each State by the Legislature
thereof; but the Congress may at any time by Law make or alter such Regulations, except as to the Places of chusing Senators.

The Congress shall assemble at least once in every Year, and such Meeting shall be on the first Monday in December, unless they shall by Law
appoint a different Day.

Section. 5. Each House shall be the Judge of the Elections, Returns and Qualifications of its own Members, and a Majority of each shall constitute a
Quorum to do Business; but a smaller Number may adjourn from day to day, and may be authorized to compel the Attendance of absent Members, in
such Manner, and under such Penalties as each House may provide.

Each House may determine the Rules of its Proceedings, punish its Members for disorderly Behaviour, and, with the Concurrence of two thirds, expel a
Member.

Each House shall keep a Journal of its Proceedings, and from time to time publish the same, excepting such Parts as may in their Judgment require
Secrecy; and the Yeas and Nays of the Members of either House on any question shall, at the Desire of one fifth of those Present, be entered on the Journal.

Neither House, during the Session of Congress, shall, without the Consent of the other, adjourn for more than three days, nor to any other Place
than that in which the two Houses shall be sitting.

Section. 6. The Senators and Representatives shall receive a Compensation for their Services, to be ascertained by Law, and paid out of the Treasury of
the United States. They shall in all Cases, except Treason, Felony and Breach of the Peace, be privileged from Arrest during their Attendance at the
Session of their respective Houses, and in going to and returning from the same; and for any Speech or Debate in either House, they shall not be questioned in
any other Place.

No Senator or Representative shall, during the Time for which he was elected, be appointed to any civil Office under the Authority of the United States,
which shall have been created, or the Emoluments whereof shall have been encreased during such time; and no Person holding any Office under the United
States, shall be a Member of either House during his Continuance in Office.

Section. 7. All Bills for raising Revenue shall originate in the House of Representatives; but the Senate may propose or concur with Amendments as on other Bills.

Every Bill which shall have passed the House of Representatives and the Senate, shall, before it become a Law, be presented to the President of the United States;

IDEA FROM HISTORY

Due process has to do with the government promising to work within the law. This idea dates back to a **document** from 1215 called the Magna Carta. It said everyone, even the king and government of Great Britain, had to follow the law.

Make the GRADE

The United States started as **colonies** of Great Britain. Colonists believed due process was so important that they made it part of the Bill of Rights.

signing the Magna Carta

THE FIFTH AMENDMENT

The right to due process is found in the Fifth Amendment. The amendment says in part: "No person shall be . . . **deprived** of life, liberty, or property, without due process of law."

Make the GRADE

The Fifth Amendment **protects** citizens from the government taking **private** property without paying the owner for it, among other rights.

Fifth
Amendment
life
liberty
property

In general, "life" means the way a person chooses to live. "Liberty" means a citizen's freedom. "Property" has to do with what a person owns, such as a house or car. The meaning of these words has been further interpreted over time.

Make the GRADE

To interpret means to explain the meaning of.

FROM FEDERAL TO STATE

When the Bill of Rights passed in 1791, it guaranteed citizens' rights when dealing with the federal, or national, government. In 1868, the Fourteenth Amendment passed. It gave citizens "equal protection under the laws." This made the Bill of Rights apply to state governments too.

White House

Make the GRADE

The Fourteenth Amendment made all people born in the United States—including those who had been **enslaved**—citizens.

FAIR FIRST

The Fifth and Fourteenth Amendments don't say the government cannot take away "life, liberty, and property." They say fair **procedures** must be followed before punishing people in a serious way. This commonly means holding a hearing of some kind before a judgement is given.

Make the GRADE

To punish means to make someone suffer. When it comes to the law, this may mean a person must pay a fine or go to jail.

Other rights in the Bill of Rights, such as the right to a jury trial, may be part of fair procedures. Federal and state laws say how a person accused of, or blamed for, a crime should be treated. Following these laws is part of guaranteeing citizens' right to due process.

Make the GRADE

A jury is a group of people that have been chosen to decide a court case. A trial is the meeting in court at which decisions are made by a jury or judge.

THE TOP COURT

The Supreme Court is the highest court in the United States. It decides cases having to do with interpreting the Constitution. If a citizen doesn't believe they have been given due process, their case may reach the Supreme Court.

Make the GRADE

The Supreme Court can decide a law or government action is unconstitutional, or doesn't follow the Constitution. Its decisions have shaped the right of due process.

U.S. Supreme Court building

The Supreme Court decides whether the government has followed the Bill of Rights and other laws. It decides whether the government has been as fair as it can be. However, the meaning of what "process" is "due" to citizens has long been hard to explain.

Make the GRADE

A court case about due process is always about how the government acted against a citizen or group of citizens.

CASE BY CASE

Whether a citizen has been given due process is decided based on individual grounds. This means there isn't one process that fits every situation. For example, a doctor losing their **license** wouldn't have the same due process as a student in trouble at school.

Make the GRADE

In 1967, a Supreme Court decision said juveniles, or people under age 18, are guaranteed the right to due process just like adults.

JUVENILE DIVISION

Judge Henry Friendly wrote some important guidelines that the government may look to when trying to guarantee due process. There are 10 points on his list. One point says to let a person know action is going to be taken and why.

Make the GRADE

The Supreme Court introduced a way to weigh both government and citizens' interests in due process cases in 1976. It's called the Mathews test and has five parts to it.

Judge Henry Friendly

DUE PROCESS TODAY

Supreme Court decisions have **expanded** the right to due process. One decision said citizens can't be deported without a hearing, because it would deprive a citizen of their liberty. Other decisions have expanded property to include driver's licenses, some government jobs, and more.

Make the GRADE

To deport someone means to make them leave the country, even if they don't want to.

The Supreme Court has decided many due process cases in the last 30 years. Many have had to do with detaining, or holding, prisoners. The right to due process has been called flexible, or easily changeable. It's likely more interpretation will happen in years to come!

Make the GRADE

The Bill of Rights was written more than 230 years ago. It's still protecting citizens' rights today!

COUNTY
JAIL

Did the government take action on a citizen?

Was there a hearing before action was taken?

Was the citizen told why action was taken?

QUESTIONING DUE PROCESS

Was the citizen able to present **evidence** of their side?

Was the decision of the hearing given in writing? Did it say why the decision was reached?

Did the citizen have a lawyer to help them? A lawyer is a person whose job it is to guide others in matters of the law.

If the answer was "yes" to all these questions, it's likely a citizen was granted due process. But it's important to remember that every due process case is different!

Glossary

colony: Land owned and controlled by another country. The people who live in a colony are called colonists.

deprive: To take something away from.

document: A formal piece of writing.

enslaved: Having to do with being owned by another person and forced to work without pay.

evidence: Something that helps show or disprove the truth of something.

expand: To get larger and looser.

guarantee: Promise.

license: A piece of paper that allows someone to do something.

private: Belonging to one person or group.

procedure: A set of steps taken to do something.

protect: To keep safe.

For More Information

Books

Brown, Don. *We the People!* New York, NY: Amulet Books, 2022.

Kaul, Jennifer. *The Bill of Rights: Asking Tough Questions.* North Mankato, MN: Capstone Press, 2021.

Website

Bill of Rights
https://bensguide.gpo.gov/bill-of-rights-1789-91
Check out this short guide to all the amendments included in the Bill of Rights.

Index